T0113887

The
WORD
in
SONG

LEWIS EVERETT

WESTBOW
PRESS®
A DIVISION OF THOMAS NELSON
& ZONDERVAN

WestBow Press books may be ordered through booksellers or by contacting:

WestBow Press
A Division of Thomas Nelson & Zondervan
1663 Liberty Drive
Bloomington, IN 47403
www.westbowpress.com
844-714-3454

ISBN: 978-1-6642-7547-8 (sc)
ISBN: 978-1-6642-7546-1 (e)

Library of Congress Control Number: 2022915158

Print information available on the last page.

WestBow Press rev. date: 09/14/2022

I will be glad and rejoice in Thee: I will sing praise to Thy name, O Thou most High.

—Psalm 9:2

CONTENTS

INTRODUCTION

Thy word is a lamp unto my feet, and a light unto my path. Thy Word have I hid in mine heart that I might not sin against Thee.

—Psalm 119:11, 105

In today's world, where things are constantly changing and shifting about, in a day and time when life can be so very uncertain, it is reassuring to know that there is still one place where we can find not only secure footing but can also know for certain we stand on solid ground. That place of certainty is in the Word of God!

I pray your whole inner being will be touched with the penetrating truth of God's Holy Word and that you will be uniquely blessed and inspired as you sing *The Word in Song* (Ephesians 5:19).

How Excellent, O Lord!

Text: Based on PSALM 8:1~4
Music: LEWIS EVERETT

1

Last time to ⊕ Coda (Msr. 36)

Div. S.A.T.B.

name is; how won - der - ful___ Thy name in all_____ the

earth!_____ O__ earth!_____ When I con -

sid - er the heav-ens, the works of Thy hands; the moon and the

stars which Thou or - dained;_____ Such awe-some pow'r and maj - es-

3

In honor of: John BJ Hall, long-time friend and brother in Christ.

Let Us Exalt His Name!

Text: PSALM 34:1 & 3
Music: LEWIS EVERETT

Open the Gates!

Text: PSALM 117:19 + 122:1
Music: LEWIS EVERETT

glad   when   they   said   un - to   me,   let us   go   in-to   the   house   of   the

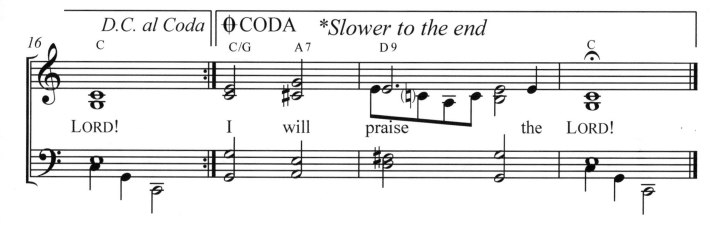

LORD!   I   will   praise   the   LORD!

Lift Up Your Hands

Text: PSALM 134:2 + 63:4
Music: Lewis Everett

morn-ing;____ Faith-ful and True, and for - ev-er the same,

Thus will I lift up my hands in Thy name!____

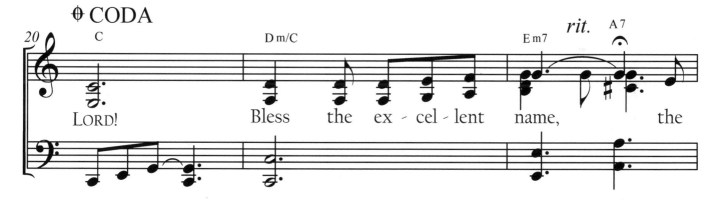

✠ CODA

LORD! Bless the ex - cel - lent name, the

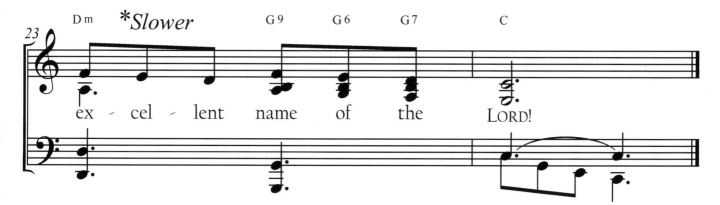

*Slower

ex - cel - lent name of the LORD!

For Stephenie: my wonderful wife, companion and very best friend!

My Light & My Salvation

Text: PSALM 27:1 & 3
Music: LEWIS EVERETT

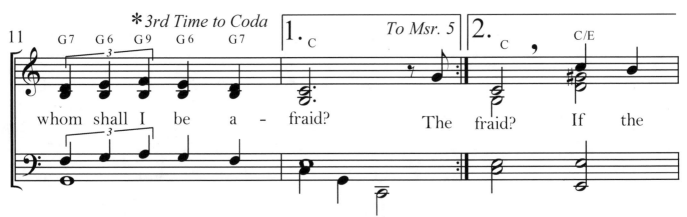

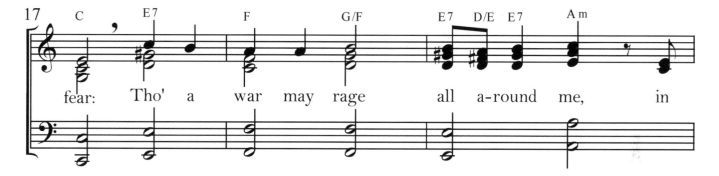

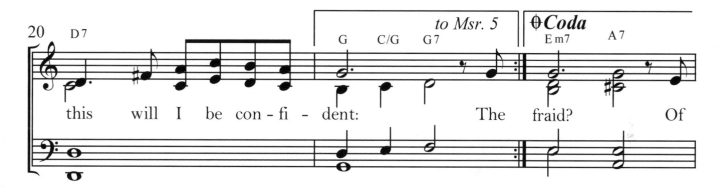

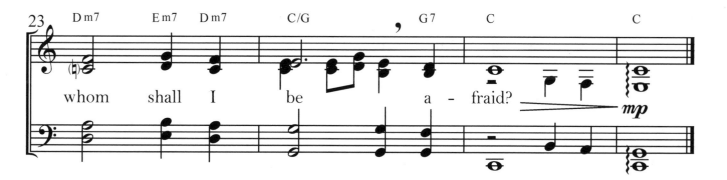

I Will Not Be Afraid!

Text: from PSALM 3
Music: Lewis Everett

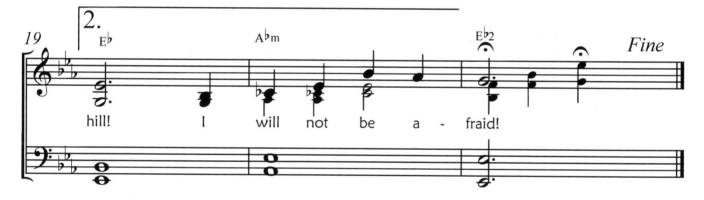

In loving memory of Regina Folger

Song of Praise

Text: PSALM 146:1 - 2
Music: Lewis Everett

In an easy-flowing manner

Merciful God

Text: PSALM 67:1
Music: Lewis Everett

16

Have Mercy Upon Me

Text: PSALM 51: 1, 2, 3
Music: Lewis Everett

Search Me, O God

Text: PSALM 139:23~24 + 86:5
Music: Lewis Everett

Prayerfully

18

A Clean Heart

Text: PSALM 51:7, 9, 10
Music: Lewis Everett

Prayerfully
♩ = 78

Purge me with hys - sop and I shall be clean.____

Wash me and I shall be whit-er than snow. Hide Thy face

from my sins, blot out all mine in-i-quit-ies. Cre-

ate in me a clean heart!___ Cre-ate in me a clean heart! O

GOD, re-new a right spir-it with-in me.____

The Forgiveness Factor

Text: EPH. 4:32 + COL. 3:13
Music: Lewis Everett

20

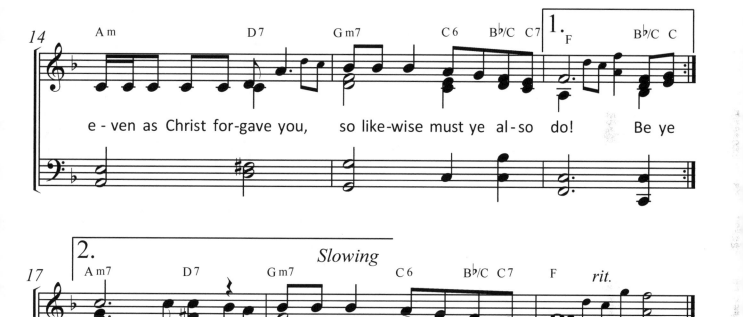

Walk In the Light

Text: 1 JOHN 1:7
Music: LEWIS EVERETT

22

He Is Faithful and Just

Text: 1 JOHN 1:9
Music: Lewis Everett

23

A New Creature

Text: 2 CORINTHIANS 5:17+21
Music: Lewis Everett

Whom Will Ye Serve?

Text from: JOSHUA 24 & DEUT. 10
Music: LEWIS EVERETT

God~Honored

Text: JOHN 12:26
Music: Lewis Everett

All for Good

Text: ROMANS 8:28 (NASB)
Music: Lewis Everett

And we know that God caus-es all things to work to-geth-er for good to those who love God, to those who are called ac-cord-ing to His pur-pose, all things work to-geth-er for good! And we know that good! Yes, all things work to-geth-er for good!

*Repeat as desired

*Last time   Slower

Our Place of Rest

Text: MATTHEW 11:28 -30
Music: Lewis Everett

We Shall Be Like Him

Text: 1 JOHN 3:2 (KJV)
Music: Lewis Everett

The Crown of Life

Text: JAMES 1:12
Music: LEWIS EVERETT

33

Life Eternal

Text: JOHN 10:10 / 14:6 / 17:3
Music: Lewis Everett

ON - LY true God and Je - sus Christ. This is life e - ter - nal, ___

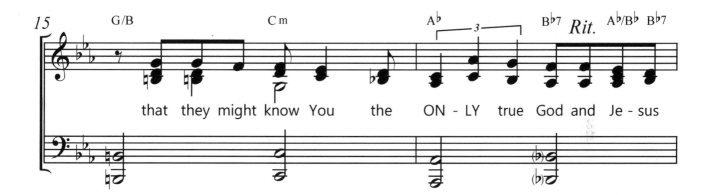

that they might know You the ON - LY true God and Je - sus

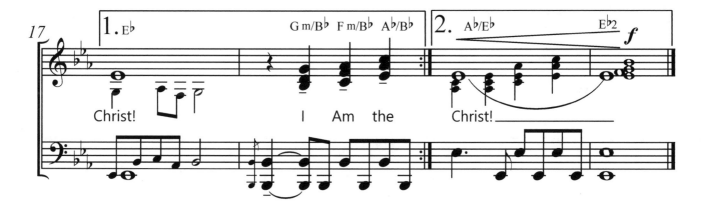

Christ! I Am the Christ! ___

Mull This Over!

Text: PHILIPPIANS 4:8
Music: Lewis Everett

Fruit of the Spirit

Text: GALATIANS 5:22, 23, 25 & 16
Music: LEWIS EVERETT

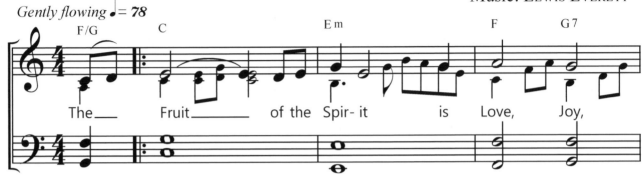

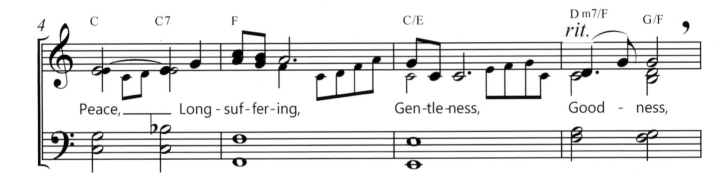

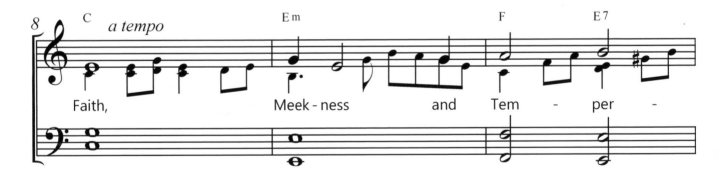

live___ in the Spir-it, let us walk al-so___ in the Spir-it. If we

walk in the Spir-it we will not ful-fill the lust of the flesh! The___

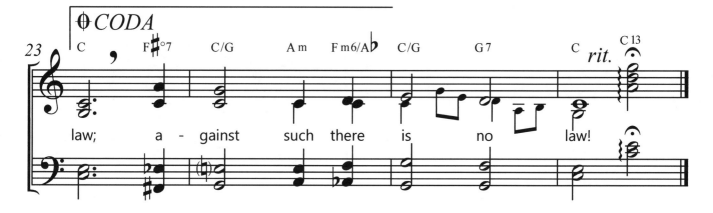

law; a - gainst such there is no law!

Saved by Grace!

Text: EPHESIANS 2:8~9
Music: LEWIS EVERETT

Call Unto Me

To: David Wayne Everett, my one and only "favorite" brother.

2 CHRON. 7:14 + JEREMIAH 33:3
Music: LEWIS EVERETT

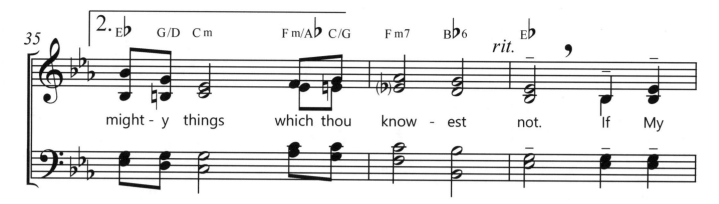

With My Whole Heart

Text: PSALM 111:1
Music: Lewis Everett

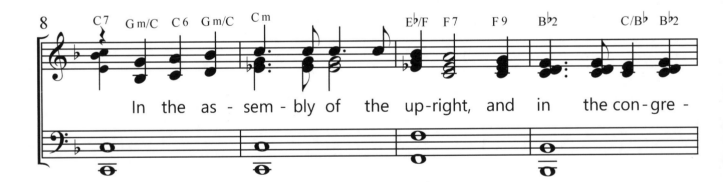

Love One Another!

Text: 1 JOHN 4:7 + 11
Music: LEWIS EVERETT

Jude's Benediction

Text: JUDE 24 & 25
Music: Lewis Everett

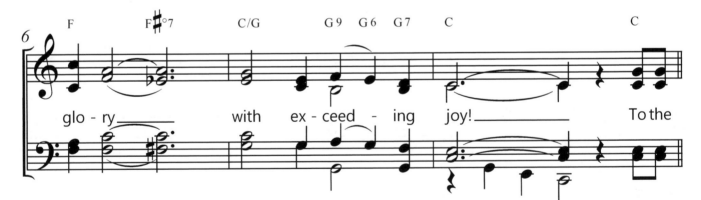

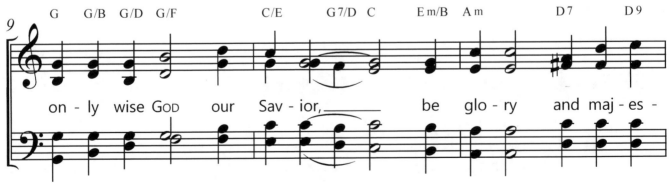

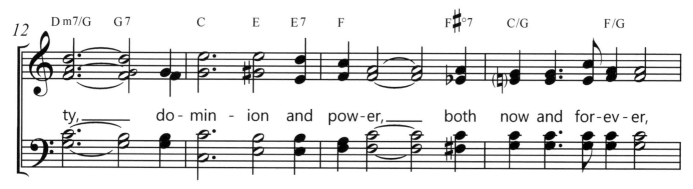

ty,___ do-min-ion and pow-er,___ both now and for-ev-er,

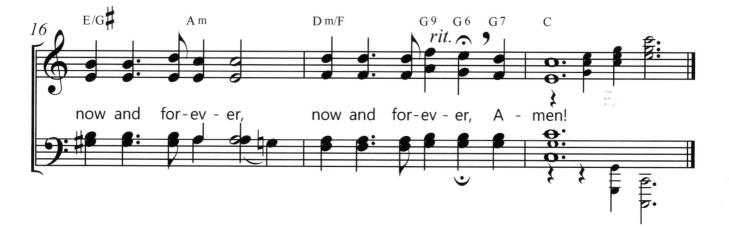

now and for-ev-er, now and for-ev-er, A-men!

ABOUT THE AUTHOR

Lewis Everett yielded his heart to the call of God, which led him down the path of church music ministry. He earned a BA in music education from Southeastern Oklahoma State University and worked as a public school music teacher for two years before moving into his first full-time church music director position; more than five decades later, he is still an active music director.

Printed in the United States
by Baker & Taylor Publisher Services